Annika Smethurst is a Walkley Award-winning journalist. She is the *Daily Telegraph*'s and *Sunday Herald Sun*'s political editor.

Writers in the *On Series*

Annika Smethurst

On Secrets

hachette
AUSTRALIA

hachette
AUSTRALIA

Published in Australia and New Zealand in 2020
by Hachette Australia
(an imprint of Hachette Australia Pty Limited)
Level 17, 207 Kent Street, Sydney NSW 2000
www.hachette.com.au

10 9 8 7 6 5 4 3 2 1

 A catalogue record for this
book is available from the
National Library of Australia

NATIONAL
LIBRARY
OF AUSTRALIA

ISBN: 978 0 7336 4499 3 (paperback)

Cover design by Luke Causby, Blue Cork
Text design by Alice Graphics
Typeset by Kirby Jones
Printed and bound in Australia by McPherson's Printing Group

I.

It was red wine that did it. A large stain on beige carpet that I had tried to fix after a bottle of Tahbilk shiraz exploded off my wine rack and onto the floor. With some advice from a carpet cleaner-turned-MP, I had managed to transform the blood-like splatter into a light blemish. It was far from the only soirée-induced flaw in my rented Canberra apartment, but it needed to be fixed if I ever wanted my bond back. As with most meetings in my life, appointments are scheduled during bouts of procrastination at work and then quickly forgotten. That morning, on 4 June 2019, I had completely unremembered arranging for a cleaner named Phil to pop over to assess the damage.

It was around 9.00 am and I was about to rush out of the door to Parliament House just 2 kilometres away when I heard the knock at my apartment door. Like that initial explosion of the shiraz bottle, my memory was jolted into remembering. 'That must be the cleaner,' I thought. Without hesitation, or my usual peek through the peephole, I opened the door. But it wasn't Phil[1], it was five members of the

---

1 Phil would arrive after the police.

Australian Federal Police who had a warrant to raid my home.

In the weeks leading up to this unexpected visit, I had rarely been at my apartment. The 2019 election campaign and interstate media commitments had meant I'd spent about 10 nights at my home in the past two months. But on that morning, 4 June, I was there. Perhaps through covert means, luck or just better diary management, the police also knew I would be home to meet the cleaner that morning. There on my landing, three male and two female police officers in plainclothes introduced themselves. For a law-abiding citizen like myself, I had assumed such an early morning visit from the police would mean a member of my family had perished in a tragic boat accident or something equally horrific. Thankfully that wasn't the case.

Shock has erased the first few words they said to me. I recall an identification badge being thrust in my face, closely followed by a warrant to search my home. Manners and fear prevented me from putting up a fight, so I let them in. Since that day I have often wondered why I wasn't bolshier or less cooperative. I am a journalist; it's in our nature. After all, this was my home and I am not a criminal. But I had been brought up to trust the police and obey their orders, so I invited them in. I genuinely believed they would ask a few questions and they'd be on their way.

There was a precedent for such things. Back in 2008, legendary press gallery journalist Laurie Oakes had revealed then-Prime Minister Kevin Rudd had ignored advice from four departments that his proposed FuelWatch scheme might push petrol prices up, not down, as it was designed to do. Under his plan, petrol stations would need to nominate and lock in prices for 24 hours. Oakes was leaked confidential Cabinet submissions prepared by the Finance Department, the Department of Resources and Energy, the Industry Department and the prime minister's own department, criticising the scheme. The leaker clearly had access to such high-level documents that even Oakes said he initially questioned the authenticity of the material[2]. The Government couldn't risk more secrets being revealed so the head of the prime minister's department, Terry Moran, ordered the police to try and identify the leaker. In 2008, Oakes wrote:

The AFP Deputy Commissioner Tony Negus interviewed me over the phone yesterday. All very civilised.

Oakes: I don't think I've got anything to say that could help you, Tony.

AFP: Are you prepared to tell me whether you are still in possession of the document?

Oakes: I'm not in possession of it.

---

2   'Fuel leaks blow up in PM's face' – Laurie Oakes, 31 May 2008, *The Daily Telegraph*.

AFP: No. Well, obviously there are circumstances around which we might have to take some kind of action, if that was the case. But if you're telling me that you're not in possession of it, then that's fine.

Oakes: The document I had does not exist anymore.

Unfortunately, when the police arrived at my apartment more than 13 months after I wrote an article revealing a proposal to expand the powers of a spy agency, I was not warned. In fact, the AFP made a decision to begin investigating the leak on 8 May 2018[3]. But the

---

3   Questions on Notice for the Australian Federal
    Police, Inquiry into the impact of the exercise of law
    enforcement and intelligence powers on the freedom of
    the press Submission 21 – Supplementary Submission.

first time I was contacted was when a squad of police arrived at my front door.

Perhaps it was a survival mechanism, but on that day my brain wouldn't let me think about the impact this raid might have on the days, months and years to follow. I somehow miscalculated the significance of what was happening and even tried to explain to the police that a man named Phil was coming over to give me a quote for some cleaning and it'd be inconvenient to cancel, as they had suggested.

I invited the police inside and we sat around my dining table, which was covered in Liberty print cotton that I was using to make two patchwork quilts for friends who were expecting babies. I like to think that this was the first time the raid squad at the AFP had to navigate their way around rotary cutters and floral fat quarters. Before June 2019, unpaid parking tickets were probably going to be the only reason I might end up in front of a judge. In my youth, I once pinched a 1-kilogram tin of beetroot from the venue where my friend had her 21st, because it seemed like a naughty thing to do with my mates. My mum had got wind of this unsophisticated stunt and made a policeman – who was a family friend – call me and scare me away from a life of crime. According to the police, it hadn't worked.

Once the AFP knew I was home they called two more policemen – IT experts – to come to my apartment. Inside, I was handed a copy of a story I had written more than a year ago and reproduced the warrant which appeared to give the police permission to search my property, my car, my phone and my computer.

Australia's secrecy laws were first drafted in 1914 after the outbreak of the First World War, due to fears of German espionage. There are two offences that make it illegal to disclose official secrets which the police seemed to be alleging I had done. Section 70 makes it illegal for a former or current government worker to disclose any information or documents they are under a duty not to disclose. The second section, section 79, lists a range of documents and items that can constitute an 'official secret'. According to the warrant:

On the 29 April 2018, Annika Smethurst and *The Sunday Telegraph* communicated a document or article to a person, that was not in the interest of the Commonwealth, and permitted that person to have access to the document, contrary to section 79(3) of the Crimes Act 1914, Official Secrets.

That subsection makes it a crime for any individual to communicate an official secret and carries a penalty of jail. The words and references to war-time acts of parliament danced on the page as my mind raced about what could possibly be in my house or on my phone that would be of interest to the police. I could feel adrenaline surge through my body, a feeling I can only recall happening once or twice before. My hands started to shake but I didn't want anyone to see. I could hear the sound of my heart beating in my chest and wondered if my unwanted house guests could also hear the accelerating thump. I couldn't possibly go to jail, could I?

According to the warrant, the police wanted notes, storyboards or scribblings – my words, not theirs – relating to an article published in *The Sunday Telegraph* a year earlier, which revealed a proposal to allow our own military spies at the Australian Signals Directorate (ASD) to spy on Australians within Australia, not just foreigners as had always been the case. At the time I knew this article caused a stir among political circles, but more than a year had passed. We had a new prime minister, there had been an election and a new Parliament was about to start.

There is huge value in knowing what you don't know. And that morning I knew I needed help. I asked to make a phone call. I had been given advice early in my career about what to do if the police ever showed up, most of which I had forgotten. But I knew I needed a lawyer. With the police just metres away I spoke to my deputy editor who was at the school uniform shop with her children in Sydney. As soon as I told her the police were at my house she responded, 'Is this about that story you wrote last year?'

'Yes,' I replied.

I called my partner who was in a meeting and diverted my call to his message bank, so I sent him a text: 'The police are here to raid my home.' I tried calling my parents to let them know what was happening before they saw it on the news. It didn't work. News of the raid was passed on to our senior legal counsel at News Corp, who called me from the gym where she'd been working out. It appears no one except the Australian Federal Police anticipated the raid on my home that morning. News Corp, my employer, sent two Canberra-based lawyers to my house to provide legal representation and moral support. I will never be able to thank these two kind and professional people for the support they provided me that day.

Moments before the lawyers reached my door the police started the search. In a strange sign of respect that conflicted with what was about to happen, the two female officers were assigned to search my bedroom from top to bottom. My bedding was removed and cupboards emptied. The two officers meticulously explored the contents of my underused handbags, reuniting me with long-lost lipsticks and unsuccessful TAB receipts from modest bets placed during the Spring Racing Carnival. I couldn't watch but then I couldn't look away. I would briefly walk into the room and justify whatever item they were looking at, like I needed to explain to the police why I had so many scarves or why I had kept a Paris metro ticket from a school exchange program in 2004.

Beside my bed I kept a small wooden box where I stored cards and handwritten notes that I had received over three decades. Inside there were birthday cards from friends, romantic notes and letters from loved ones who had since died. I had failed to appreciate how the significance of personal correspondence is lost when shared with people beyond the writer and recipient. Medical scripts, diaries and photos kept in the sanctuary of my own home were being read and looked at by people I didn't know.

As is now committed to the annals of Wikipedia, the police also searched my undies drawer. As Sky News host Laura Jayes said on-air at the time: 'Never has there been so much focus on one journalist's underwear drawer.' Much has been made about this in the media, but it was far from the worst thing to happen that day. Would you prefer strangers look through your bras and briefs, or the contents of your bathroom cupboard and private text messages?

In my kitchen another policeman inspected my oven, on the off-chance I had stored secret documents in my grill for the past 13 months. It felt perfunctory, and therefore deliberately intimidating. The same feeling engulfed me when the police searched my freezer and my bin. What did they think they would find in my kitchen bin, which only contained food scraps and wrappings from the past few days? For more than seven hours the cops riffled through my laundry basket, looked inside my shoes and in the pockets of all my clothes. Items in my pantry were pulled out one by one. The police untangled Christmas lights and poked around my baubles in search, I can only assume, for some kind of state secrets.

Old newspapers I had kept from the start of my career as a reporter in regional Victoria were inspected, page by page. I can only assume they were looking for any notes I may have made in the margins. The police opened an old folder where I kept shorthand notes from my journalism cadetship. It was one of many items I had forgotten existed. I told the police to leave it out as I would ditch it after they had left. The raid had transformed into something of a law-enforcement-style Marie Kondo experience.

The squares of floral fabric, which were still on my dining table, were gently inspected one by one and placed back in the pattern I had designed. One officer made small talk and asked about the patchwork tools I used to cut out the squares. Oddly I obliged. I explained that by using a rotary blade I could cut the squares faster. I never finished those quilts. Cookbooks – more than 50 of them – had each page examined. One officer was inspecting a recipe book by Israeli–British chef Yotam Ottolenghi. He said he had given his wife the same one as a gift and asked me what my favourite recipe was. Again, I obliged[4]. Another policeman who was rooting around my living room commented on the Collingwood Football Club magazine on my

---

4   The rhubarb and strawberry crumble cake in *Sweet*
     by Yotam Ottolenghi and Helen Goh on p.148 is
     delicious.

coffee table and discussed my team's chances in the finals.

At the time, I accepted that these interactions were to cheer me up during an uncomfortable situation for all involved. But in moments of scepticism I suspect it was a trick – which is also used by journalists – to warm up the subject for further questioning. Perhaps the policeman hoped our conversation would naturally move from the lucky third-term mark West Coast player Elliot Yeo took against Collingwood in the 2018 Grand Final, to how I learnt the Australian Government wanted to spy on its own citizens.

Watching strangers rummage through my modest but homely apartment was horrible. It was the first place where I had lived alone, free of housemates or family. This humble Canberra apartment had become my private retreat, a sanctuary from some of the more public aspects of my job. Not anymore.

I was also forced to hand over the passcode to my mobile phone. At the risk of further damaging the reputation of millennials, giving police access to my iPhone – and therefore my text messages, search history and screenshots – filled me with incredible anxiety. It might not sound like a hardship and doesn't deserve comparisons to the horrifying violence inflicted by some countries on journalists, but this was an incredible intrusion. It didn't just expose police to my private thoughts and opinions, but to the secrets my friends, family, colleagues and contacts chose to trust me with.

It should come as no surprise that on my phone were the phone numbers of, and messages from, hundreds of politicians, staff and other political apparatchik. It's how we do our jobs. Weeks before the raid, Radio National presenter Patricia Karvelas had been roundly criticised for reading a text message live on ABC's *Insiders* from Barnaby Joyce denying any involvement in negotiations on water buybacks. Viewers screamed that the very fact she had his number showed some kind of bias or cosy relationship. This outrage seemed strange to me. Calling and texting pollies is how we get the information to tell the public what is going on. The very business model of a journalist requires sources to trust us with information, with their secrets. Sometimes strangers who wish to expose wrongdoing also get in touch and need to know their secrets are safe. Journalism isn't simply about exposing everything we know without a filter, as some people would believe. It takes time and trust.

After handing over my iPhone, the police copied the entire contents of the handset onto a computer. For hours they sifted through text messages, photos and notes using keyword searches and time stamps, in search of anything that might be relevant to their investigation. At one stage the police thought they had found some gold in an old text message exchange and asked me to re-enter my password after my phone automatically locked. It wasn't a state secret, it was a photo of a not so aesthetically pleasing politician being compared to a friend's ex-wife. I was mortified and swore off such nastiness in the future.

I sat, legs crossed, on my kitchen bench next to the sink, as it was the only space that wasn't being pulled apart by the police. I could hear my phone dinging with alerts as news of the raid made its way around the world. I was trying not to cry. I had wanted to keep it all a secret because I didn't want to worry anyone, least of all my family and friends. It was too late for that. I have always been a people pleaser. I have always been afraid of letting others down.

One of the few smiles I get when I think about the day my home was raided is my naivety. I thought, or perhaps hoped, it would all be over in an hour, that no one would find out and I could get on with my day. Phil would give me that quote to repair the stain on my carpet and I'd make lamb for dinner. I'd slip back in to work and perhaps tell a few people in the coffee queue about the day the police popped into number 46. Labor leader Anthony Albanese wouldn't go on TV to talk about my underwear drawer, I would continue living in my apartment and the full bench of the High Court would never need to consider Smethurst v. Commissioner of Police.

This naive narrative I had was in direct contrast to what was unfolding. Within 30 minutes of the police arriving at my home I had media on my front lawn and had been contacted by *The New York Times* and a book publisher (the one who published this book). Politicians, friends and family members called as the news was broadcast across Australia. I knew I had lost control of the situation when a message of support arrived from Isabel, my French host mother who lives in the small town of Luçon in the south Vendee region of France. I lived with Isabel and her family 15 years ago as an exchange student at high school. She had seen the story on the news. 'Tout notre soutien et notre amour pour cette épreuve. Bon courage. Bisous,'[5] she wrote. The cat was well and truly out of the bag.

It was a freezing day in Canberra, which is not unusual for June. Even with two heaters

---

5   'All our support and love for this test. Good luck. Kisses.'

running and 10 people in my apartment, it was cold. We were also hungry. Perhaps it was mild Stockholm syndrome or my life-long quest to be a good hostess, but I decided to join the search. Not for secrets but for sustenance. My cupboards were almost bare in a post-election way that only press gallery journalists or political staffers will understand. But, at the back of my pantry, I found some old packets of almonds and peanuts. I poured them into bowls and offered them to my unwanted house guests. As I say, I am a people-pleaser but what was I thinking offering snacks to the people invading my privacy?

The sun started to drop and the lights went on. Neighbours in my apartment block returned home from work only to be greeted by hordes of reporters. Then, after seven hours, the raid was over. Again I sat at my dining table, only this time I was surrounded by seven police officers and two lawyers as they showed me the text messages which had been removed from my phone and copied onto a USB stick. The most senior officer intervened to delete a few text message exchanges I had with Labor's Richard Marles and Murray Watt after the story was published. Then they were gone.

It was still and silent and I cried until I had no more tears left. I couldn't watch the news or turn on the radio – a symptom which lasted for an inconveniently long period of time for a journalist. I didn't want to take calls from anyone because I wasn't sure I could pretend it was going to be ok. I just wanted to undo that day. I wanted to hide under my doona so that is what I did.

II.

Legendary US newspaperman William
Randolph Hearst often told his editors, 'News is
something which somebody wants suppressed:
all the rest is advertising.' It's an oft-used and
regularly muddled quote in journalism circles
that is meant to remind us what we are here to
do. As reporters we must expose secrets and tell
the truth to readers. We are here to scrutinise

the Government and hold the powerful to account. It's an essential part of our democracy.

Admittedly that doesn't always happen. Every journalist wants to break big yarns but they are not easy to find, and sometimes the public aren't always that interested in the things journalists find interesting. As well as breaking news, journalism is often referred to as the first draft of history, so it's also important to cover government announcements and daily events. Not all news has to be exclusive and not all news has to be bad news. Despite this, most journalists like to break stories rather than follow them even though readers rarely care who revealed the story first.

A lot is made about whether stories are in the public interest or whether it's just that the public are interested. Sex scandals are a classic example. When Barnaby Joyce was exposed for leaving his wife to have a baby with a staff member, readers fell into one of two categories. Either they believed the story was salacious gossip and it didn't matter what Joyce or any other pollie did after hours. Then there were those who accused the press gallery of a cover-up for not writing about the worst-kept secret in town earlier. Regardless, the story sold papers and subscriptions and had eyeballs glued to television news. Politics and policy may be important to some, but stories about crime and sex tend to sell newspapers. Beautiful women don't hurt either, which is why UK paper *The Sun* has persisted with running near-naked ladies on page three for so long. In Australia we are a more prudish bunch and you are more likely to see cute kids or animals on page three, but it's a popular part of any edition. There is no point being highbrow about it. Politics is rightly boring to many Australians.

In 2013 I wrote a story in Melbourne's *Herald Sun* exposing provocative and inappropriate number plates which had been banned, including DUMSHT and MYNOB. So popular was this story that I did a follow-up in 2014 when a man named Trevor wrote to then-Premier Denis Napthine demanding the number plate I♥DYX be removed from the road. Seven years on, I still receive at least one email a month about the naughty number plate story. To date I have received far more emails about those crude number plates than I ever received about a proposal to expand spying powers, which triggered a raid on my home.

That article was published in April 2018 under the headline 'Spying Shock: Shades of Big Brother as Cyber-security Vision Comes to Light'. It revealed that two government agencies were discussing a proposal to expand surveillance powers for Australia's electronic spy agency, ASD. Stories like this require a lot of research. I knew the story had to be told, but convincing people to talk to me about this policy area was tough. It was also important to explain to readers why they should care about increased surveillance powers. When you see a car with a smutty number plate you can understand why you might get mad. But Australia's network of spooks operates in the shadows and many Australians take the view that if you haven't done anything wrong then there's no reason to worry about people spying on your bank accounts or text messages.

To understand the significance of this yarn, it's important to know what was being proposed. As one of six security and intelligence agencies, the ASD plays a crucial role in gathering foreign intelligence. Its primary role is to defend Australia from global threats. Think of a tech-savvy James Bond fighting Russians, but from a laptop.

After the end of the Second World War, the Federal Government ticked-off on a new peacetime signals intelligence organisation. The ASD formally came into existence in 1947 when it was known as the Defence Signals Bureau. Since then, its purpose has been to track down and disrupt cybercriminals outside Australia, not threats from within. The digital spies at the ASD are meant to abide by the motto, "reveal their secrets and protect our own".

By law, the ASD can obtain intelligence about foreigners. Nothing in Australian law gives the spies at the ASD the right to access private data on a computer located inside Australia, even if doing so would thwart a crime. Traditional boundaries don't always apply in cyberspace, so the agency presumes that people inside Australia are Australians and those abroad are not, unless there is evidence to the contrary. It is up to the Australian Security Intelligence Organisation (ASIO) as well as state and federal police to snoop on Australians who are up to no good here.

The article published in *The Sunday Telegraph* revealed Department of Home Affairs boss Mike Pezzullo wrote to the Defence Secretary Greg Moriarty in February 2018, outlining a proposal to potentially allow the Government's own military hackers to snoop on Australians.[6] The departments had even outlined scenarios where our cyber spies would use online tactics to counter or disrupt

---

6   'Spying shock: Shades of Big Brother as cyber-security vision comes to light' – Annika Smethurst, 28 April 2018, *The Sunday Telegraph*.

cyber criminals both onshore and offshore. Mr Pezzullo said the move could help battle child exploitation networks and transnational criminal syndicates including terror networks, both at home and offshore. He argued traditional law enforcement, done by police and ASIO, didn't have the technical capacity to detect and disrupt organised crime and instead Australia was forced to depend on foreign partners.

Home Affairs had advised Defence it would brief its minister, Peter Dutton, and ask him to write to Defence Minister Marise Payne seeking her support to whip up legislation to expand the powers of the ASD. These conversations were happening as Parliament was debating legislation which would make the ASD an independent statutory agency, forcing it to be more transparent. At the time that legislation was being reviewed, Margaret Stone, the Inspector-General of Intelligence and Security – the spy agency watchdog – looked at the Bill and warned against further changing ASD's focus beyond the proposed legislation.

'Nothing in the Intelligence Services Act would allow ASD to access restricted data on a computer physically located inside Australia – even where doing so would assist in gathering intelligence or disrupting crime,' Stone's submission said.

Accessing data located inside Australia is properly an action that requires an ASIO or police warrant.

A change which extended the immunity or which changed ASD's focus for its covert or intrusive intelligence related activities to people and organisations inside Australia would be a profound one.[7]

It is the belief of many figures within the intelligence community and Parliament that Stone was using veiled language to sound a serious alarm. Many people didn't support this move, including cabinet ministers.

Finding sources for any story can be difficult; stories that involve security agencies are even harder. I have vowed never to reveal my sources, so the lengths I went to research this yarn will remain one of my secrets.

7   Intelligence Services Amendment (Establishment of the Australian Signals Directorate) Bill 2018, Submission to the Senate Foreign Affairs, Defence and Trade Legislation Committee – The Hon Margaret Stone, Inspector-General of Intelligence and Security.

The day before the story was published, the details of the article were put to the Government and initially denied by a media advisor for Defence Minister Marise Payne. The two departmental secretaries and ASD Director Mike Burgess issued a public statement denying any plans to covertly access Australians' private data but added:

> In the ever-changing world of cybersecurity as officials we should explore all options to protect Australians and the Australian economy.

Despite their denial, I had done my research and I knew it was right. But when you send a story like this to the printing press the dominant emotions are always dread and anxiety. Millions of eyeballs will see your words and you have to back yourself. After she was appointed a Member of the Order of Australia, investigative journalist Kate McClymont perfectly explained the emotions journalists experience as their work is sent to be printed.

'When you do have a major story, the night before you just feel physically ill,' she said. 'You don't feel a sense of joy or victory or anything like that, you just feel sheer fear ... because the stakes are really high.'[8]

---

8 ‘“You just feel physically ill” – Kate McClymont on a career of exposing Sydney's dark secrets’, 25 January 2020, *Sydney Morning Herald*.

The day after my story was published, Home Affairs Minister Peter Dutton said there was a 'case to be made' for expanding the powers of Australia's cyber spies.

'In relation to terrorism the Government has otherwise introduced a number of legislative measures, but I think there is a case to be made [for further changes],' Mr Dutton said. He continued:

There has been an elevation in terms of the toolkit that investigators have at their disposal if they are investigating a terrorist-related incident. The argument is whether or not there should be enhanced arrangements for people fighting these criminals, particularly in the child exploitation space.

But many of Dutton's colleagues on Cabinet's national security committee – including then-Prime Minister Malcolm Turnbull and Foreign Minister Julie Bishop – did not support the change. When asked about the proposal the next day, Ms Bishop said there was no need for the reform and responded with a firm 'no' when asked directly if senior public servants wanted to expand the role of the ASD to spy on Australians.

'The current laws safeguard the privacy of Australians but also provide us with an opportunity to keep Australians safe ... I don't see any national security gap and I certainly believe the current laws safeguard the privacy of Australians but also keep Australians safe,' she said. 'I take my advice from our security and intelligence agencies and they have not raised with me any issue that would require an expansion of ASD powers such that you would use them against Australians.'

The story had exposed a rift within Cabinet. After a restless night I went out for brunch with some friends. By lunchtime the Defence Department had referred the leak to the AFP. Labor also called for an investigation the day the story was published, despite screaming for leniency when my house was raided. Shadow Attorney General Mark Dreyfus wrote to then-Prime Minister Malcolm Turnbull encouraging him to call in the police. 'Leaks such as this risk damaging the integrity of the work these agencies do, and raise questions about your Government's competence and credibility on national security,' he wrote.

III.

A good yarn is only ever as good as its source. Sources can come from anywhere. Sometimes information is provided by anonymous whistleblowers who see wrongdoing and wish to expose it. Sometimes strangers will write you letters or emails or pick up the phone and cold call a newsroom. Some sources are friends or family members; others are professional contacts and get in touch after you build trust.[9] Sadly, there is a growing trend among journalists to try and reveal a competitor's alleged source. Instead of following a story and trying to get a new angle, some reporters try and discredit an article by attacking the source of the information. In the current environment, journalists have enough challenges and readers should be sceptical of any journalists who take this path.

It's true that not all sources are reliable, that goes for information from Cabinet ministers too. Journalists must ask why a source has decided to share information and what they want in return. A whistleblower may have political motivations.

---

9   A lesson for young journos: Always, always be nice to the secretaries who answer the phones as they are more likely to pass on good tips.

That doesn't mean the information is wrong, it just needs to be considered. Malcolm Turnbull lost his authority, and ultimately the Liberal leadership, after senior Treasury official Godwin Grech fabricated an email that alleged then-Prime Minister Kevin Rudd gave special assistance to an Ipswich car dealer in return for the use of a free ute. The opposition appeared to have a solid leak and used the email and Mr Grech's evidence in a Senate inquiry to demand Rudd stand down. But the email was revealed to be a fake.

In my career I have received tip-offs from primary school friends, politicians and taxi drivers. When former health minister Sussan Ley was under pressure for buying a property on the Gold Coast during a work trip, she insisted the $795,000 purchase was 'unplanned and unanticipated'. Her defence was destroyed when a retired couple revealed Ms Ley had twice inspected their rural property, and made an unsuccessful offer months earlier, when also in Queensland for work. The couple cold called the newsroom to see if we were interested to know that Ms Ley and her partner had arranged an early morning inspection because she had to fly back to Canberra. They didn't want anything in return and they didn't have an agenda.

Some of my colleagues have received the most amazing tips in Ubers or from school parents standing on the side of a kids' sports game. Often the best tips come to you over drinks at the pub. A close friend and colleague was out drinking one night when he received a tip-off that Ford was about to close its Australian manufacturing plants. The paper had gone to print but he wrote the note down and put it in his pocket. The next morning 3AW's Neil Mitchell broke the news on-air and went on to win a Walkley for the scoop.

In the public imagination, sources tend to take the form of 'Deep Throat' – the anonymous government source who leaked secret information to the *Washington Post* reporters Carl Bernstein and Bob Woodward, which brought down President Richard Nixon in the Watergate scandal. Woodward said he would arrange meetings with Deep Throat – later revealed as FBI agent Mark Felt – by putting a red flag in a flowerpot on his apartment balcony that was visible from the street. Sadly, I have never reached this level of creativity with a source, but technological advancement means it is more important than ever for journalists to have face-to-face conversations with people and avoid online communication.

At a fraud conference in 2018, Kate McClymont revealed she once received a secret letter at work asking her to arrange for a smiley face to be printed on the weather page of the *Sydney Morning Herald*. Doing so would send a signal to the source that she would like more details about a house purchase made by former NSW Labor politician Eddie Obeid that he wanted to keep secret.

After winning the 2019 Gold Walkley for their reporting into the Lawyer X scandal, the *Herald Sun*'s Anthony Dowsley and Patrick Carlyon revealed the story started from a tip-off, which turned out to be wrong, during a boozy pub lunch with police. But the faulty information led Dowsley to uncover gangland lawyer Nicola Gobbo had been recruited as a secret police informer.

And sometimes it's more cock-up than conspiracy. In 2018, the ABC got its hands on hundreds of top-secret and highly classified Cabinet documents found in two old filing cabinets sold at a Canberra shop which sells ex-government furniture. There was no key and the documents were only discovered when the bargain hunter opened the cabinets with a drill.

In 1980, three-time Walkley award winner Laurie Oakes published the guts of the federal budget two days before budget day, in one of the greatest political leaks of all time. Recalling that leak, Oakes said he met his source in a hotel car park on a Sunday morning. He handed over then-Treasurer John Howard's speech which he was due to deliver in two days' time. Oakes grabbed his tape recorder and read the entire speech into the microphone in 15 minutes, while his contact ducked off for a quick drink. Such a meeting might be harder to arrange these days, with our digital footprint leaving a trail of data. Oakes may have returned Howard's speech to his source, but other journalists have grappled with what to do with documents. One retired reporter told me his children once innocently threw leaked Cabinet papers on a bonfire in their backyard. Another colleague told me he had taken notes he had made from a now-retired Cabinet minister to his elderly parents' house and dug a hole in their backyard in suburban Sydney. I am still not sure his parents know what was buried deep in their garden bed.

Although the raid on my home was rare, it is not without precedent. In 2004, the office of Investigations Editor for *The Australian* Natalie O'Brien was raided by the AFP searching for leaked internal ASIO documents that alleged a US intelligence liaison had warned the Federal Government about specific terrorism activity likely to happen in Indonesia in the lead up to the Bali bombings.

In 2008, the AFP raided the home of Canberra reporter Philip Dorling, for a second time, looking for material linked to a story that China, North Korea and Japan were priority targets for Australian intelligence.

In 2016, during the election campaign, the Australian Federal Police raided the Melbourne office of former Communications Minister Senator Stephen Conroy and the home of a Labor staffer as part of an investigation into damaging leaks regarding the National Broadband Network. More recently, the AFP raided the Adelaide home of tax office employee Richard Boyle who was a key whistleblower in an investigation into the extensive powers of the tax office.

I believe these stories exposed secrets the public deserved to know. Our democracy relies on brave sources or whistleblowers exposing the truth and trusting journalists to tell these stories. As it stands, it is an offence to communicate some information the government wants to keep secret. Journalists are given some protections through a 'journalism defence' if the information is found to be in the public interest. This so-called safeguard is not enough. In some cases, this defence may help journalists stay out of jail, but there are very few protections for public servants who see wrongdoing and wish to expose it. Without equal protection for sources who wish to speak the truth, journalism is not protected.

Whistleblowers, such as Jeff Morris who exposed corrupt practices at the Commonwealth Bank and tax office debt collector Richard Boyle who spoke to journalists about dodgy debt collection practices, risk everything to expose dark secrets. Most of us like to think we would report misconduct or wrongdoing if we saw it, but studies suggest the majority of Australians would turn a blind eye. Despite our convict heritage, Australians tend to hesitate before standing up to authority and can be hostile towards those who dob. Whistleblowers are often perceived as troublemakers or squealers. Perhaps it's our propensity not to dob in a mate that stops us from speaking up.

Researchers from Griffith University's Centre for Governance and Public Policy found that in 97 per cent of cases, whistleblowers first raised issues internally with their employer, giving the business or agency a chance to right a wrong. The study found that, on average, whistleblowers report concerns to regulators or integrity agencies about 16 per cent of the time and fewer than one per cent of whistleblowers talk to journalists, and then only after trying internal or regulatory channels first.

Those brave enough to speak out are rarely thanked for their community service, instead they often face reprisals and punishment for doing the right thing. If former Commonwealth Bank employee Jeff Morris didn't speak out against corrupt practices by financial planners there never would have been a royal commission into the banking sector. Mr Morris initially tried to raise his concerns with corporate watchdog the Australian Securities and Investments Commission (ASIC) before going to the press, frustrated by years of 'dithering'.

In 2017, Morris made an incredibly raw submission to a parliamentary inquiry into whistleblowers detailing the enormous toll he had paid for speaking up:

> The financial cost of being a whistleblower is generally severe. Although I agree with Churchill's comment that the basis of human morality is doing what is right, regardless of the consequences, that didn't help me to answer my now 12-year-old son when I told him, not for the first time, that he couldn't have something he wanted and

he riposted, 'Dad, why did you have to be a whistleblower?' The automatic connection between being a whistleblower and financial sacrifice is one that even a child can make.

Aside from the immediate loss of employment you are affected in two ways that makes it difficult to recover financially. The stress you have suffered and the revulsion at what you have seen as a whistleblower makes it difficult to "fit in" to an organisation again. Normal can never be normal again. Even when you think you are ready to move on, smear campaigns can make it difficult to obtain employment in your industry.

Part of the cost of being a whistleblower is the impact on your family. Most whistleblowers wind up losing their family.

Obviously the stress, financial impact and effect on the family are all interrelated in a somewhat vicious circle.

In my case my wife was opposed to me blowing the whistle on CBA from the beginning. Her refrain was that they would destroy me and then what would happen to her and the kids? Many times over the years she asked me why I was doing all this for people we didn't know.

Certainly under the current system hers is a reasonable viewpoint. It is very hard to justify the price you and your family must pay to do the right thing. In fact, you cannot justify it rationally, only morally.[10]

---

10   Submission to joint parliamentary inquiry into whistleblowing by Jeff Morris, CBA whistleblower.

Australian Taxation Office whistleblower Richard Boyle may pay an even heavier price. The former debt collector became an internal whistleblower in 2017 before speaking to the press about aggressive debt collection practices. As a public servant Boyle faces more than 160 years in prison if convicted.

For people like Boyle and Morris who are willing to risk their careers and freedom, journalists want to be able to provide an unfettered assurance that they will be safe. Sadly, it's impossible. Journalists may be willing to go to prison for refusing to reveal a source, but that is not enough protection. Metadata from phones and other surveillance techniques make it incredibly difficult to preserve anonymity. Short of putting a red flag in a flowerpot on your balcony, few lines of communication are completely safe. Media organisations often encourage whistleblowers to use online tools like SecureDrop, which encrypts documents so that not even the recipient will know where it comes from. End-to-end encrypted messaging apps like Signal or temporary burner phones may also offer added protections, but most journalists agree that avoiding a digital trace is the best way to communicate.

This level of protection will be necessary until Australia increases protections for those who try to expose wrongdoing. I believe the raid on my home was about more than evidence gathering. It sent a message to would-be whistleblowers not to speak up. Now, when someone observes a potential abuse of power they might hesitate before exposing the truth. Australians deserve better laws that protect journalists and whistleblowers who want to expose secrets that should be told.

IV.

I was on the way to Ikea when I heard about a second raid at the ABC the day after my apartment had been turned upside down by police. The Australian Federal Police chose the morning after the raid on my home to search the public broadcaster after hundreds of pages of secret defence force documents revealing allegations of potential war crimes by Australian Special Forces in Afghanistan were leaked. According to court documents, the AFP was searching for evidence that could prove investigative journalist Dan Oakes had committed the offences of receiving stolen goods and unlawfully obtaining military information. That warrant allowed police to search for and record 'fingerprints found at the premises' and to take samples for 'forensic purposes'. The big difference was the ABC had been warned the police were coming so they could arrange swipe card access to let them in.

The exposure of the past 24 hours had taken a toll. I had attempted a self-imposed media blackout, but had caught the start of a news bulletin about the ABC raids when the car radio automatically switched on. I needed an antidote to my acceleration into the spotlight. A mundane activity to get me out of bed and focused. The night before I had asked what sort of jail sentence I could potentially face in a worst-case scenario. I was told two to five years. I distinctly remember thinking two years might be manageable, which isn't true. It's funny how we trick ourselves as a method of coping. Perhaps two years could be spent reading, or writing a book. I even started to think how nice it would be not to have to worry about dinner or what to wear each day. Perhaps I would become a powerlifter. Hopefully it would be a nice jail in regional Australia. One where I would help rehabilitate injured wildlife, not make number plates.

Just 24 hours earlier, that bloody shiraz stain was weighing on my mind, now it was incarceration. Ikea was the only answer. Being trapped in a maze of flat-packed Swedish furniture might seem like an odd way to relax, but on that day I needed the structure and order that their diagrams and Allen keys provided.

I had also made a very quick decision never to spend another night in my apartment again. It might sound dramatic but the world now knew where I lived and I harboured an irrational – or perhaps very rational – fear that my home was bugged. An anecdote from a colleague who shivered outside my home during the raids also solidified my decision. As photographers lingered on my lawn a passer-by yelled out, 'So that's where Annika Smethurst lives.' I was out.

I would move in with my partner – a raid-triggered cohabitation. Who said romance was dead? But that would mean I needed somewhere to keep my clothes. I wasn't yet in jail and I still had a collection of dresses that needed storing. Instead of reading newspapers, which featured photos of my home, I trawled the Ikea catalogue in search of the perfect project to take my mind off jail. Would my family visit? How often?

The now-discontinued Trysil wardrobe, in dark brown, with sliding doors and drawers was going to be the reason for getting up that day. Since June, I have often laughed at the absurdity of deciding to put together an Ikea wardrobe during an already stressful situation. Friends have suggested that maybe a massage or a boozy lunch might have been a better choice.

Months later, I relayed this to a psychologist who was helping me deal with the ongoing stress of the court case. I felt validated when she said the repetition and methodical nature of putting together Ikea furniture was probably the best thing I could have done to cope with overwhelming stress. Especially for A-type personalities like myself who are often ambitious, rigidly organised and like to be in control. On 5 June, I was none of those things. In fact, I was so panic-stricken that the police would return and comb through my things that I took a bag of birthday cards from the wooden box and barbequed them on the Weber so no more strangers could read them.

Perhaps one of the worst consequences of being raided and pursued by the police for doing my job was that it shook my unwavering determination to be a journalist. I was born a few years before the 'recession we had to have' as Treasurer Paul Keating famously labelled it. At a very young age I surprised my parents by parroting that famous line. For as long as I can remember I have been interested in politics and wanted to be a journalist. At Girton Grammar School in Bendigo, my homeroom teacher Mr Lorincz once told me he wasn't surprised I had wanted to study journalism. This wasn't because humanities subjects were my strong suit, but because I was nosey. He pointed out that I always knew what time school assembly was held, which teachers were moving on to another school and who had detention. I have often relayed this to journalism students who ask me what skills you need for a job in the media. Curiosity is the answer.

But since 4 June my confidence in sticking to journalism has waned. I have often asked myself, What is the point? An evaluation of the risk-versus-reward didn't seem to add up. I had worked hard to expose the truth and I could lose my freedom. I knew I had hit rock bottom when I found myself googling horticulture courses or considering applying for a job at the doggy day care where my new puppy occasionally stayed[11]. I know I am not the only journalist to have these thoughts. I recently spoke to seven-time Walkley award winner Hedley Thomas about the intimidation and threats journalists in Australia have faced for doing their job. In 2002, Thomas, who was working as an investigative journalist for *The Courier-Mail*, was lying in bed with his wife, Ruth, when several shots were fired at their Brisbane home. One pierced the wall of his children's toy room. Another had come within centimetres of his wife.

No one goes into journalism for a lucrative pay cheque or to make friends. In fact, if you do your job correctly, you will always anger

---

11 Merv the dalmatian arrived a few weeks after my house was raided and can be credited with keeping me sane.

someone. Early morning phone calls from angry pollies or media advisors are the norm and don't cause too much grief, but sometimes it becomes personal.

At the end of 2018 I was in the meat section of Woolworths buying supplies for a barbeque when a text message arrived from a National Party staffer saying he hoped my 'family dies of vicious cancer. I mean that painful cancer for a vicious feminist C***'. The message was in response to a story I had written about his boss, Senator Barry O'Sullivan, who had been demoted on the LNP senate ticket ahead of the election. Thankfully this type of aggressive and nasty language isn't normal, nor are home raids. But the collective brutality of that year took a tremendous toll.

Initially, it was the sound of a doorbell that caused a rush of anxiety. Shortly after my home was raided and I had moved to a new suburb, there was a buzz at the door. My partner had forgotten to tell me a plumber was coming over to fix a faulty gas meter. I froze at the sound, terrified as to who would be on the other side. It took many months but I am now comfortable opening the door and that's a milestone I never thought I would need to celebrate.

Other things have been a lot harder to overcome. After 4 June 2019 I woke up each morning knowing there was a possibility I could be arrested and even go to jail. I didn't know when or if it would happen but the threat was always there. Colleagues reassured me it wouldn't happen, which is exactly what I would do in the reverse situation. But despite countless opportunities to do so, the AFP and the Government refused to rule out charging me.

Every day I would wake up full of ambition that today would be a normal day, but the story was everywhere. I turned on the TV one morning to hear Home Affairs Minister Peter Dutton defending penalties for journalists, which included jail. Speaking from London where he was due to meet the Queen, Scott Morrison was asked if he was concerned that a journalist's home had been raided and he replied, 'It never troubles me that our laws are being upheld.'

The media attention was relentless and gave me an insight into what those on the other side of the lens face when we report on their lives. It's been a tough but valuable lesson which I hope serves me well in the future.

With publicity came conspiracy theories. A member of the public even tried to access information about my private life using freedom of information laws. As a journalist I have interviewed people who have been thrust into the media spotlight, sometimes it's a choice or due to a fabulous achievement, but often it's through unexpected circumstances. I learned the hard way that infamy is awful.

In order to survive I had to restrict my media consumption, which was not only limiting professionally but also denied me something I have always loved. Even comedy shows became off-limits when Shaun Micallef from the ABC's *Mad As Hell* began cracking gags at my expense. I banned my family and close friends from talking to me about work. It felt as if nothing else in my career had mattered and people only found me interesting because I might go to jail. There were pledges of support and promises to protest and shut down Parliament if I was charged. These offers were kind, but I have never felt more alone.

One Tuesday night in November I was reading a book in bed when a friend sent me a link to a story about U2 frontman Bono opening his Australian tour by backing Australia's press freedom campaign. 'Truth is the bedrock ... and journalists are its guardian angels,' he said. *Bono* for goodness sake.

I was standing at a luggage carousel at Sydney airport when I learned human rights lawyer Amal Clooney had also joined the fight, criticising the media raids because they could be used by leaders of more oppressive countries as an excuse to crack down on press freedoms.

Perhaps if these celebrity interventions had resulted in an invitation to George Clooney's 18th century villa on Lake Como or Bono's Killiney mansion I might have been more enthusiastic. In reality I felt isolated and I wanted it all to go away.

If using flat-pack furniture as a relaxation technique seems absurd, then purchasing a new puppy during one of the most stressful periods of my life will sound laughable. But that is exactly what I did. Merv the dalmatian arrived in July. As a breed, dalmatians have a reputation for being loyal, playful and thrive on human companionship. The toilet training and chewing might have added to my stress, but the friendship and routine gave me a reason to live. It may sound dramatic but I felt under such enormous pressure in those first few months that I would fantasise about, and even plan how, I would disappear. I would picture myself driving for miles and miles and starting a new life. A quiet life. But Merv had to be walked twice a day. It got me out of the house and it was in these moments that I would briefly stop thinking about my own legal woes.

Annoyingly, in those blissful moments when I did manage to forget about jail, I was often jolted back to reality by members of the public approaching me, mostly with messages of support. One night at the pub, with a make-up free face and covered in dog hair, I was approached by three blokes who asked if I was the girl who was raided. They offered their support and expressed outrage at what had happened, but I just wanted to be ignored. Weeks later Merv and I walked past a man on the street who made a joke about where my other 100 dalmatians were hiding. We had a short chat about dog breeds and it felt normal. A few days later he emailed me saying he had recognised me and that's why he stopped to chat. This happened at airports, the dry cleaner and even in Vietnam where another tourist asked if I was 'that journalist' facing jail. When I was collecting a wine order from the post office I whispered my name to the lady behind the counter and she loudly responded, 'No wonder you need wine given what you are going through.' I smiled. I just kept smiling.

The support was always appreciated but I never got used to strangers having opinions on my life. Why let the courts or police decide if you have broken a law when talkback callers and the bloke at the petrol station have the answer? I have also learned a lot about Australians and how we use humour as a defence mechanism, often to avoid talking about serious issues that make us uncomfortable. Jail jokes, I have heard them all. There has not been a single day since June 2019 that someone hasn't cracked a joke about the prospect of me losing my freedom. 'Haven't they locked you up yet?' is the most popular one and has been thrown my way by both strangers and senior politicians in the halls of Parliament. I also get asked if I am being followed or, oddly, whether I am wearing underwear, which just makes no sense. One day I wore a forest green jumpsuit to Parliament and an MP made a remark that I was already dressing for prison. Apparently these are the things you say when you don't know what to say. Again, all I could do was smile and hope the world wouldn't see how terrified I really was.

I don't believe these remarks were ever intended to hurt me but it has taught me how to speak to anyone facing adversity. When a very senior Labor MP cracked a joke at my expense I reflected on how insensitive it would be for me to mock him or his party's election loss. I am not seeking sympathy as my woes pale to insignificance when compared to other hardships people face every day, but we often dehumanise people caught up in scandal. There is always a human side. This is a lesson which I know will help me as a reporter. I understand the cynicism the public has towards journalists and I am willing to face the consequences of my actions. But I simply miss my old life and still mourn what I have lost. A psychologist told me that I may never get that old life back and I was crushed.

There is an immense guilt I feel for people inadvertently caught up in this mess.

Politicians often refer to their parents, children or partners as conscripts, and I agree. Nobody wants to be the cause of stress for their loved ones. In 2007, *Herald Sun* journalists Michael Harvey and Gerard McManus were convicted of contempt of court after publishing a story which revealed the Commonwealth's plan to clampdown on veterans' entitlements. Harvey and McManus are incredible men and have offered me guidance and support during my legal battle. Understanding the prolonged stress felt by loved ones during such an uncertain time, Harvey was the first person to ask how my mum was. He told me his own mother attended his court case and burst into tears when he and McManus were warned about the possibility of going to jail.

Perhaps one of the hardest things I have had to deal with is the attacks on my professionalism. Senior government officials, police and department heads trying to undermine my story have repeatedly challenged my professionalism on a mission to discredit my work. These attacks are written into Hansard and will never be erased. For the most part, I have ignored these accusations of poor journalism, publicly at least. But it has always struck me as strange that Mr Pezzullo described my report as 'erroneous' and 'false' when *The Sunday Telegraph* quoted a letter that he later told a senate hearing he knew 'intimately'.

More recently, in February 2020, Peter Dutton made it clear he would support the proposed reforms to the ASD, saying:

ON SECRETS

What I think is that there should be a
public debate about whether we think it's
acceptable for our society to tolerate the
presence of these criminal networks right
next door to us and yet we have no ability to
do anything about it.

V.

Newspapers are imperfect. Every day we arrive at work to an empty book with some sections blanked out for ads, which pay for our product. Reporters pitch up yarns and battle for a good space. We do checks to ensure accuracy. We argue about the merits of the stories and editors battle for a mix of different articles to please the public. Sometimes an unexpected event like a natural disaster pushes your copy to a less prominent place. Newspapers, while imperfect, are imperative.

To me, press freedom always sounded like a great concept, but not one that I would ever have to worry about. Like human rights or democracy, it was something I valued but took for granted. I now know how impossible it is to truly appreciate something until it is denied to you. But if journalists struggle to get excited about press freedom, it's an ever harder task to rev up the public about the need for greater protections for the press.

One of the roadblocks we face in exciting the public about press freedom is that journalism, as a vocation, is often misunderstood. In 2019 the Australia Talks National Survey asked

54,000 Australians what professions they trust the most. Doctors and nurses were trusted by 97 per cent of survey responders and police by 84 per cent, while only 54 per cent of people surveyed said they trusted journalists. It might be higher than the number of people who trust pollies, union leaders and celebrities, but this distrust makes it difficult to mount support for our work.

On the top of my Twitter feed I have a GIF of Hyacinth Bucket – or 'Bouquet' if you were to ask her – from the BBC sitcom *Keeping up Appearances*. It's there, not only because I adore the series, but because Hyacinth is asking 'Where's the press?' I posted it in 2017 when a Twitter user complained that the mainstream media was ignoring revelations that Health Minister Sussan Ley had bought a holiday house while on a taxpayer funded trip to the Gold Coast. Except, of course, the media hadn't missed this story. It was broken by me and followed up for a week by my newspaper and colleagues in the press gallery until Ley stood down. A certain sector of the community – primarily those on social media – had falsely assumed the story had originated on Twitter and not in a newsroom.

Sadly, this tale is not unusual. Through no fault of their own, many people don't understand how professional journalism differs from other content that appears online. Trust in news organisations continues to plummet and there is now an unwavering cynicism towards news outlets where an entire profession is now judged by its worst practitioners.

Every election cycle the lack of media literacy is on display when newspapers endorse candidates in elections. Typically this appears in the days leading up to polling day, as an unsigned editorial on the opinion pages that supports one candidate. It's been happening for more than a century and is meant to offer a summary of a party's promises so readers can make up their own minds. It doesn't mean that the newspaper will only ever endorse one political party, or that every journalist votes the same way. It also doesn't stop newspapers being critical of members of the endorsed party. But every single time this happens people are seething. They are usually the same people who get angry when news is behind a paywall because they want journalism to be free. It's not the fault of voters that they don't always understand or agree with how journalism works, but it makes it difficult to expect them to support a campaign for free press.

The second problem is trust. Results of a survey, released the same month my house was raided, revealed Australian's trust in traditional and digital media had rapidly declined in the past five years, mainly due to fears of 'fake news' and doubts about the intentions of media outlets. The poll found that trust in print publications such as newspapers and magazines had dropped by 14 per cent in five years while trust in TV and radio news had declined 13 per cent. Alarmingly, more than half of those polled believe there is far too much 'fake news' in newspapers and magazines. The stories that fill newspapers might sometimes be overblown, or sometimes you don't agree with them, but this shouldn't be confused with 'fake news'.

But it appears some readers and viewers have become so confused by disinformation campaigns that they have allowed it to undermine their faith in the whole media industry. Whether driven by foreign actors or so-called citizen journalists, disinformation and hoaxes have become a legitimate way to discredit news by the mainstream media.

While governments should promote media literacy, many Australian politicians are following Donald Trump in using the term 'fake news' to discredit their critics. Poor reporting should always be called out, but when politicians weaponise the term 'fake news' against journalists they dislike, it can be dangerous for democracies.

Barack Obama's former communications director Dan Pfeiffer talks about this in his *New York Times* best-selling book *Yes We (Still) Can*. Pfeiffer argues that the term 'fake news' is being used by politicians to describe any information that is inconvenient to them. Pfeiffer explains the efforts he went to disprove a conspiracy theory that Barack Obama wasn't born in the United States. The rumour started in email chains that journalists refused to cover because the allegation wasn't true. It eventually made its way into mainstream news and Obama was forced to release his full birth certificate to the public. Pfeiffer writes:

> Years later, four in ten Republican voters still believed that Barack Obama was not born in the United States. And it's not that they didn't know about the birth certificate that was released; it's that they refused to believe it.
>
> If the mainstream media said it was real then the mainstream media was lying to cover up for Obama.

In this 'post-truth' era facts appear to be optional and trust in the media is a dwindling commodity. Multiple studies have also found that people are more likely to believe news if it comes from someone they know personally than from a politician, journalist or news outlet. This implosion of trust isn't just a problem for the media, but for charities, businesses and governments too. The only way to restore faith in the media is to encourage legitimate journalistic endeavours that expose wrongdoings that the Government would otherwise cover up.

In late October 2019, Australia's major media organisations put down their swords to call for reforms to protect public interest journalism. Australia's Right to Know coalition includes the Nine Network, News Corp, the ABC, SBS, *The Guardian*, and journalists' union the Media, Entertainment and Arts Alliance. The strength of the coalition lies in its unity. Most of the time media organisations and their journalists ruthlessly compete for stories, allowing the Government to divide and conquer. In order to protect journalists and whistleblowers the entire industry needed to come together to campaign for change.

I had just returned from much-needed leave when the Right to Know campaign was launched. In an unprecedented move, Australian's biggest newspapers agreed not to compete for one day and redacted all of their front pages in a protest against press restrictions. It was a powerful symbol that received global attention. That week, media bosses Michael Miller from News Corp as well as Nine's Hugh Marks and the ABC's David Anderson also addressed the National Press

Club to call for six changes that would level the playing field for Australian journalists. They argued that the current laws have turned journalism into a crime and limit our ability to hold the powerful to account. Marks used the 'boiling frog' metaphor to warn about the dangers of gradual change.

Monash University Associate Professor Johan Lidberg has found more than 60 new laws and amendments relating to Australia's national security that have been introduced since the September 11 terror attacks – an international record. No one questions the need to protect Australian citizens, that is the primary task of any government, but Australia now offers fewer protections to journalists than other Western democracies. This fear of the truth in Australia poses a threat to our democracy.

The changes being sought by Australian media organisations aren't unheard of and would bring Australia into line with many Western democracies. It was up to the full bench of the High Court to decide whether the warrant used to raid my home was properly drawn up. We believe media outlets should have the right to challenge a warrant against a journalist before the raid is conducted. This would avoid the need for a lengthy, stressful and costly legal fight.

Other changes include stronger protections for public sector whistleblowers and rules governing what information governments can mark secret, with a commitment to regularly audit the material being kept from the public. Australian media organisations also want exemptions that would protect journalists from prosecution under national security laws for public-interest journalism. Improvements to the Freedom of Information Act for quicker and easier access to government documents, as well as updated defamation laws are other requested changes.

I understand the public cynicism in giving more power to an already unpopular press but these reforms will without a doubt improve the quality of journalism in this country and help us tell citizens what they have a right to know.

The responsibility of speaking up for something as important as press freedom is daunting and I constantly worry that I am not up to the task. I never want this to be about me. No self-respecting journalist wants to become part of the story. I never wanted to be a poster girl for press freedom, but I know it is important so I do it. It may sound overblown, but defending press freedom is defending everyone's freedom.

Read
'On'

Little Books,
Big Ideas

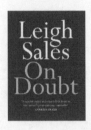

'A superbly stylish and valuable
little book on this century's great
vanishing commodity.'
Annabel Crabb

Acclaimed journalist Leigh Sales has her doubts, and
thinks you should, too. Her classic personal essay
carries a message about the value of truth, scrutiny and
accountability—a much-needed, pocket-sized antidote
to fake news.

Donald Trump, the post-truth world and the instability
of Australian politics are all examined in this fresh take
on her prescient essay on the media and political trends
that define our times.

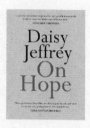

'Next-gen leaders like Daisy are showing us the way and their voices are only getting louder. We should listen.' Mike Cannon-Brookes

How ordinary people can change the world and help save the planet.

As extreme weather becomes the norm, scientists agree that our climate is changing. But it seems too many of our leaders aren't listening to the science and are failing to act.

In *On Hope*, one of the lead organisers of the Australian Climate strike, 17-year-old Daisy Jeffrey shows how ordinary people are fighting back and demanding we address climate change to help save our planet.

'This is the book we all need right now. Gemmell
nails how to achieve serenity and calm amid all the
crazy busyness of modern living.'
Lisa Wilkinson

International bestselling author Nikki Gemmell
writes on the power of quiet in today's shouty world.

Quiet comes as a shock in these troubled times.

Quietism means 'devotional contemplation and
abandonment of the will … a calm acceptance of things
as they are'. Gemmell makes the case for why quiet is
steadily gaining ground in this noisy age: Why we need
it now more than ever. How to glean quiet, hold on to it,
and work within it.

Katharine
Murphy
On
Disruption

The internet has shaken the foundations of life: public and
private lives are wrought by the 24-hour, seven-day-a-week
news cycle that means no one is ever off duty.

On Disruption is a report from the coalface of that change:
what has happened, will it keep happening,
and is there any way out of the chaos?

Don
Watson
On
Indignation

Don Watson takes us on a journey of indignation and how
it has been expressed in his forebears. His ire towards US
politicians has a new moving target: Donald Trump.

The US President's primary pitch had less to do with
giving people money or security than it was about
vengeance. Trump exploited the anger we feel when
we are slighted or taken for granted, turning the politics
of a sophisticated democracy into something more like a
blood feud. He promised to restore their dignity, slay their
enemies, re-make the world according to old rites and
customs. He stirred their indignation into tribal rage and
rode it into the White House.

It was a scam, of course, but wherever there is indignation,
lies and stupidity abound.

If you would like to find out more about
Hachette Australia, our authors, upcoming
events and new releases you can visit
our website or our social media channels:

hachette.com.au
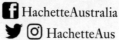